ROOTS BEFORE BRANCHES

caleb james

First published online by Wattpad, 2020

"I found solace in open love;

And, for that, I know I am enough."

TABLE OF CONTENTS:

THE ARTIST

The artist you once saw in your nightmares
was tortured; deprived of clean air.

Basements covered in violent sprays of
paint,
Mansions bought with blood money.
His art wishes he were a saint,
Consumed by a glimpse of glory.
And, his parents never did like the man he
became,
Overcome with anti-penance and a broken
spirit,
All he ever knew was shame; an unaltered
sense of weakness.

The man you see in your dreams is a
tortured artist,
Beloved in your eyes but betrayed by his
own.
His creativity is simply an envious game;
one he might forfeit.
Is this really his only way back home?

The man you see in your dreams is a
tortured artist,
A poet on the brink of brutal promise.

Literature torn at the seams,
Relationships ruined by whispers of
negativity.
Hopelessness submerges itself within his
screams,
Halting any and all chances of him reaching
his ability.
A studio resembling a mausoleum,
He can't count the amount of stories that
died here,
The bones of the books create a hollow
museum,
Once written with love but unwritten in
fear.

The man you see in your dreams is a
tortured artist,
Beloved in your eyes but betrayed by his
own.
His creativity is simply an envious game;
one he might forfeit.

Is this really his only way back home?
The man you see in your dreams is a
tortured artist,
A poet on the brink of brutal promise.

Dizzying spells of writer's block,
Characters all bleeding into one.
Is this why he feels so lost?
Has he forgotten to have some... fun?

The man I see in the mirror was once a
tortured artist,
A writer on the verge of a cursed promise.
But, after battles and struggles with
entities I cannot explain,
Lightbulbs lit and epiphanies emerged,
Something pushed away my pain,
Chaos could very well cradle courage.
This box I've lodged myself into is the most
clichéd of tropes,
A mirror image of everyone's demons;
Suicide is glamorous and death is hope.
Counteractive solutions to redundant
reasons.

I'm shedding skin I didn't even know I had,
Taking one for the team, a bullet to the
heart.
Maybe I had to go through such glorious
agony to feel glad,
I had to find my out; find my way to my
own art.
The man I once saw in my nightmares was
once a tortured artist,
On the heels of a poetic, fatal promise.

I love that I didn't know how to love what
I love,
It made me know I am enough.
I took a vow with myself in the mirror
yesterday,
I promised that as long as I have this
creative outlet,
And I have a bad day,
I'll always write poems about it,
And force the pain away.
The artist you once saw in your dreams will
be brand new the next time you fall asleep.

What The Fuck Is Going On?

News reels of nightmares I cannot wake up
from,
In the morning, I'm terrified by the sun.
I watch the numbers rise as if they'll never
stop,
Metaphorical serial killers on the loose;
only, they'll never be caught.

I'm too numb to look out my window,
I'm too scared to leave my house.
I'm too afraid of the unknown,
All I wanna do is fucking shout.

Going under,
Much to ponder.
Death is life and life is death.
I don't know what this world's come to,
Seems like kids are dying from a bad flu.

What the fuck is going on?
Did we, as a race, forget to right some God
awful fucking wrong?

I'm worried about my grandparents who
are simply too weak,
I pray to whoever's up there,
Don't force them to leave.
I'm worried about my father, who's always
had trouble breathing,
I'm worried about family friends,
I can feel everyone dying.

I'm too fearful to watch the news,
I'm too sad to face reality.
All I feel are never-ending blues,
I'm in the midst of a fucking tragedy.

Going under,
Much to ponder.
Death is life and life is death.
I don't know what this world's come to,
Seems like kids are dying from a bad flu.
What the fuck is going on?

Did we, as a race, forget to right some God
awful fucking wrong?

Someone must've fucked karma up big
time,
Nobody deserves this unnatural crime.
Lungs are burning and drowning all at
once,
Maybe there is no saving us.

Going under,
Much to ponder.
Death is life and life is death.
I don't know what this world's come to,
Seems like kids are dying from a bad flu.
What the fuck is going on?
Did we, as a race, forget to right some God
awful fucking wrong?

Fuck Off Frat Boy

AΔ
Red solo cups full of nothing but poison,
Parties you choose rather than those
chosen.
America is failing; it's rotting, it's broken.
He just uttered a threat he knew should've
went unspoken.
Ralph Lauren polo shirts you know were
bought with daddy's money,
Stilettos heels; she's trying to stay close to
eternal glory.
A sin is a sin even if it's dressed in
diamanté,
We'll never be able to cover up the pain.

I've been to parties where kids basically ask
to die,
And it scares me each and every time.
But, college parties are levels I could never
understand,
Just look where he has his hands.
I'm in overalls and an oversized red

sweater,
Enormous black frames; for my eyes they
cover.
Mr. Popular walks up to me and says with a
grin and a pill,
"I can show you how to win".
Fuck off frat boy, I don't want to mix with
you,
I know exactly what you're up to.

Parties you see in the movies are tame in
comparison,
Chandeliers are in pieces on the floor and
vomit is laying next to them in unison.
Givenchy dresses are torn at the seams,
Nightmares won't ever become dreams.
We're drowning our sorrows in Smirnoff
and Bacardi,
This is the perfectly wrong kind of party.
You may be wondering why I'm here,
I'm writing this in the spare bedroom, I can
think; it's quiet, it's clear.
Lauren is here because her boyfriend fucks
anything that moves,
Kilian is here because all he ever will do

with his music is lose.
And, me, I'm here because my mind is
failing me,
I'd rather risk it all than write some
pathetic, victimised poetry.
I have issues and problems I cannot wrap
my head around,
This party is the perfect explosion for the
silence in my head; it's unashamedly loud.

But, as I'm writing these words on the back
of scrunched up toilet paper,
I can feel something that I've never felt
before.
It may be the alcohol returning to my lips,
I cannot quiet explain this.
I leave the bedroom at 11.45,
I'm walking past friends I know I'll lose
tonight.
I leave the fraternity house with something
coming for me,
It's an idea; a renewal of poetry.
I lay on the grass next to burning Greek
letters,
I suddenly feel so much better.

I've finally cracked the code for what I've
been feeling,
Happiness is not a constant, it will always
be fleeting.
I used to beat myself up for feeling sad,
Now I know I don't need to do that.
So, thank you to the god awful shitshow I
just left,
I think you've finally made a version of me
I actually think is the best.

Boardwalk

It's the fifties, kid.
Romance is thriving, alive and well.
Just make sure we conceal everything we
did.
God only knows how heavenly we've made
this hell.
Sunsets happen so late this time of year,
Throwing a golden hue into your eyes,
You don't know how happy I am to be
here,
Even though I know, when we see the sun
again, this love dies.

Why did we get so tangled up in this?
But I have no regrets.
This love is my only wish,
Oh, how I love putting the universe to the
test.

I like kisses on the boardwalk,
I like pretending we're everything we're not.
Taking me to places I have not been,

Showing me places I have not seen.
I wonder will we ever be more than lust,
Could this paradise ever pull you in to
trust,
To trust me and the words I speak,
I promise, this secret is safe with me.

"Don't fix what isn't broken",
I've heard them say that once or twice.
But, they don't know my heart's been
frozen,
They're skating on the valves of such
delicate ice.
This is the place that was once our
boardwalk,
Where, hours on end, we would just talk.
You, about your days as a cashier worker in
the city,
And I, about my paranoia always creeping
up behind me.

Two mirror images in love,
It's more than enough,
Enough to taint the purest of the pure.
Tangled liked barbed wire in our pages that

keep on turning,
We kiss, as we laugh,
Smoke rises from their eyes burning.
Nobody wanted this to work,
So, my heart broke.

And nobody understands what we once
had,
It's what they're all looking for.
Without you, this lifetime's been a drag,
I never knew I didn't feel loved before.
We'll probably never cross paths again,
Hell, I wouldn't be surprised if you're long
dead.
It has been seventy years, after all,
But, I wish I could give you a call.
One last dance on our boardwalk would
have been nice,
It would've been closure, perfect closure to
both of our lives.

Such Sweet Horror

80s synths in my head,
A fear so heavy; it's thumping my chest.
I left campus at 8:30 last night,
I'm still on the road, full of worry, I won't
get to camp until morning's light.
I'll pull over for an hour; I need to rest.
I know I'm a coward; what's new? What's
next?

Headlights illuminate the dead of night and
rain pelts on the roof of my car,
An awful fright and a blade in my heart.
Tears mix with blood on my lap,
I've been stabbed! I've been stabbed!
Somehow I've arrived at my home for the
summer,
Darkness rages above, here comes the
thunder.
"Help me! Please, I've been attacked!",
I scream in fear,
My friends think I'm going mad.
I look down at my torso where there was

once blood,
Vacant of evil; I'm healthy where I'm stood.

Days go by after a nightmare so real,
I honestly don't know how to feel.
I'm certain I was injured, I know it for
sure.
Am I deluding myself with such sweet
horror?
There's a record player in the corner of my
room; it's bright green;
Suddenly, a song scores my doom; oh, the
villainy.
I shriek! I cry!
As I feel my heart break.
My soul is yours to take.
"It's true! It's true!"
I was bloody and hurt.
Now they'll all see a corpse coming forth.

I race downstairs cradling my insides;
I try to tell my friends that I'm dying
inside.
Once again, shock horror! They do not
believe,

That I am at an end; I am slowly dying.
There must be a serial killer on the loose;
He's taunting me with a loving noose.
Everything seems calm outside my mind,
Why the hell have I imagined such a
crimson crime?

I walk back upstairs with my sorrow and
fake smiles,
As I realise who's behind such disgusting
acts; so vile.
It's me.
I'm the killer behind the mask.
I'm the monster laying in wait in the long
grass.
I'm the enemy I've been terrified of,
I'm broken hearted; when will this stop?
I'll pay any cost.
Will I survive my summer spree?
Or will I fall at the hands of my greatest
enemy?

Oh No

Oh no, here they go.
Falling into love.

Headphones in at this hovel of a coffee
shop,
He's listening to music just to get lost.
Rats making friends with empty dinner
plates,
Kids falling in love on first dates.
And then there's him, alone with lyrics he
cannot relate to,
Yet, somehow, he still feels blue.
Steam rising from a fresh batch of
americano,
Saints in her eyes, oh no.
His music stops almost as fast as his heart,
She's a living, breathing work of art.

Is he the one?
Is she the one?
Oh no, here they go,
Falling into love.

Posters of 80s chicks plaster his walls,
He asked his mother to tear them down
before she calls.
She said she loved Taylor Swift;
Just as he did; And they bonded over it.
Births and deaths followed by funerals and
marriages,
They've been together through all of it.
A guy and a girl trying to make sense of the
world,
Just two kids who don't know where to go.

Lilac visions of what may one day come
true,
It's taken his head far too long to come to.
Everything is finally falling into place,
He thinks he can finally trust in his fate.

Singing at the top of his lungs,
Dancing on New York City rooftops.
It's about time he started having fun,
He's far too dismal when he's not.
He's laughing until his cheeks swell up,
Exploring New York City dive bars.
He's finally hearing a new song,

After replaying the same ol' shit for so long.
He's finally reading a brand new book,
Can't believe how long this took.

This love is in technicolor,
It's unique; not like any other.
When I'm down it lifts me up,
When I'm insecure it gives me trust.
I take what I can get from it,
Some kind of endorphin informant.
This love is in technicolor,
I never want to experience another.

Rosé spilled over white table cloths,
Waiters forgetting which order was ours.
Moments that never want to end,
Love blossomed between two great friends.

I'm beaming from ear to ear,
Laughing on Parisian rooftops.
I can't believe how far I've come in one
year,
I was writing books I hoped would keep me
from getting lost.
I'm trying not to cry from happiness,

Exploring Paris' dive bars.
I'm finally experiencing a love like this,
After going through the same ol' shit for so
long.
I'm finally reading a brand new page,
Can't believe how long I've been waiting for
this stage.

And I know that your heart's as fragile as a
windowpane,
And I know that all you ever knew was
pain.
I can promise you trips to Spain,
You can have everything your way.
I can promise you popcorn and dim lights,
You can have everything right.
I can promise you all I have at twenty,
Like some kind of James Dean entity.
I'd die for you.
I'd die for you.
I know this might sound extreme,
But you know exactly what I mean.
I'd die for you.
I'd die for you.

Oh no, here they go.
Falling into love.

Lightning in a Bottle

Most of the time I feel like my heart has
been shipwrecked,
Even the wind feels extremely hectic.
Other times I feel like I am empty,
If you stabbed me I simply would not
bleed,
I'm hollow; I'm fading.
Maybe it's the dire drivel of poison I create,
Or maybe it's happiness coming far too
late.
I try to smile when the clouds evaporate
and I free fall through the starless sky,
At least someone will love me when I die.

But you; you love me now.
You fix the fire in the sky, I don't know
how.
Love is too weak a word to describe how I

feel,
Thank you for making me real.

This night is lightning in a bottle,
Nostalgic Disney movies and popcorn.
Laughing until I can't catch my breath,
I know this smile is heaven sent.
It may be dark and dreary right outside,
But I am calm with you by my side.
This night is lightning in a bottle,
I could sing it's praises like an anthem.

Months pass by and I haven't had the urge
to cry,
That's a victory in itself, time for some
celebratory wine.
This may be the most chaotic of
juxtapositions,
But I am so happy right now; even when
the world is drowning in depression.
And that's all because of the airiness I feel
around you,
I feel rejuvenated, I feel reborn, I feel new.

This night is lightning in a bottle,
Nostalgic Disney movies and popcorn.
Laughing until I can't catch my breath,
I know this smile is heaven sent.
It may be dark and dreary right outside,
But I am calm with you by my side.
This night is lightning in a bottle,
I could sing it's praises like an anthem.

Stars shine brighter than they ever have,
Roses are more gorgeous than ever before.
Cheeks hurt from all of the laughs,
I could not ask for anything more.
This life is lightening in a bottle,
I can't wait to catch it; celebrating with
salted popcorn.
Sunrises, sunsets and everything in
between,
This lightning in a bottle is my everything.

Londontown

So many questions that I need answered,
So many blank pages without chapters.
Insecurities growing from the foulest of
ambiguities,
A tyrant with murderous tendencies.
Trips across a body of water,
All to change a history that may one day be
altered.
A change of pace and a brand new face,
Packaged with this antiquated place.

This is a complicated city and there's
something nice about that,
You can bring guns into the corner shop,
but - please, no hats.
I have a notebook full of wondrous
illustrations,
Full to the brim with my oldest questions.
But, one thing I've always known
throughout my life; that when I'm feeling
down;

I feel so alive in the middle of the night here
in Londontown.

A thousand miles have been racked up,
Destined to find someone I can trust.
I'm walking down such historical streets,
Streets that allowed for me to be me.
I touched grandad's wall in the park where
my father would play,
You have no idea how grateful I am for
that day.
I walked along the Thames by my favourite
restaurants,
I could spend forever here just getting lost.
This city, I know for certain, will one day
be my home,
I feel London lodged within my bones.

Half of me remains here every time I leave,
The amount of family I have here, you
would not believe.
There's magic in the history,
London is my ancestry.
Whenever I feel down and I know I'm
about to place blame,

I find myself sitting on a cold, cramped
plane,
Destined for a city I adore so much.
Every side alley and street corner; I know I
can trust.
I'll forever find love in London until the
day I die,
I'll write poetry in Earl's Court tube
station, waiting for the Piccadilly line.
I'll never complain about the crowded
trains again,
Somehow they feel like a warm, familiar
friend.
In the winter months, at 3:30pm the sun
goes down,
And suddenly, I feel so alive in the middle
of the night here in Londontown.

Shakespearean Romances

I've been unintentionally writing
Shakespearean Romances since I was
fifteen,
Writing worlds away in a desperate bit to
understand me.
I've built up characters just to write their
fall,
I know we can't have it all.
I've tried to write myself into a narrative
that simply doesn't need me,
Bruising my ego so easily.

I get so foggy sometimes,
Especially when someone new strolls into
my life. (I don't know how.)
I get so cloudy sometimes,
Especially when I start to utilise my
rhymes. (Like, right now.)

I've been unintentionally writing
Shakespearean Romances since I was
fifteen,

Writing worlds away in a desperate bit to
understand me.
I've built up characters just to write their
fall,
I know we can't have it all.
I've tried to write myself into a narrative
that simply doesn't need me,
Bruising my ego so easily.

My friends only know half of who I am,
I tied the other half to the tracks; praying
for death from the incoming tram.
Sensational fiction mirrors everything I
experience,
Art is a reflection of life; it really is.
I'm a poet and I know it,
But, fuck, some days I know I'm about to
blow it.

I've been unintentionally writing
Shakespearean Romances since I was
fifteen,
Writing worlds away in a desperate bit to
understand me.
I've built up characters just to write their

fall,
I know we can't have it all.
I've tried to write myself into a narrative
that simply doesn't need me,
Bruising my ego so easily.

I'll be damned if my story is told as a
tragedy,
People better not laugh at it like it's a
comedy.
These chapters belong in a portfolio of
romance,
One you should read, taking a chance.
I've been writing Shakespearean Romances
since I was fifteen,
Writing words with hints of me.

Shakespeare called on the classics,
Thus, he created literary magic.
Meanwhile, I'm fucking frantic,
Perilously, pointlessly panicked.
Madder than King Lear during the courts,
More broken than Hamlet but that's not
what hurts,
I've had love fizzle out faster than two star

crossed lovers,
Sadness never seemed to be over.
So I'll keep writing my Shakespearean
Romances until I can turn tragic into true,
And I can find my way back to you.

Lovely

There's a reading nook in the corner of this
countryside cabin at sunset,
This place could be creepy if it wasn't so
gorgeous.
Fresh batches of coffee fill the air,
Walking barefoot up and down the stairs.
Dancing until my feet swell up and my
body announces it's had enough.
As I'm twirling, I glance in the mirror, and
realise: happiness has never felt so good.

Just like the movies,
We are where we should be.
Isn't this lovely?

Photographs taken out of context,
Who will say "I love you" next?
Picnics in lavender fields,
Finally finding something real.
That cherry blossom candle smells so sick,

Burn it once until it has no wick.
This night is effervescent poetry,
Isn't this lovely?

I could get lost in this beautiful silence,
Nobody could find me but I couldn't care
less.
Spending my days rolling down hills,
This time last year I was swallowing pills.
How stunning can one life be?
I ask myself, expecting some cosmic answer
with a dash of irony.

Just like perfection,
I can't feel any tension.
Isn't this lovely?

We moved dinner inside tonight,
Horizons vacant of skylines,
Nothing here but wasted time.
I dream dreams just to wish them to die.
I want to be lazy; I don't have the energy to
chase my future tonight.
Skies turned grey but we love when it's
raining.

I'm romanticising everything that is
mesmerising.
I'm safe here; with the fire lighting and
some root beer,
Isn't this lovely?
Isn't this lovely?

Sunlight slips through the blinds at dawn,
Bed sheets replaying dreams; on and on.
I'll read some poetry before I have some
breakfast,
Today is a new day; a brand new chance;
A chance to be better and a chance to be
kind;
A chance to write letters full of all things
nice.
Maybe I'll send them to the people I once
loved,
I'll let them know however long we had was
enough.
I'll give closure to myself and a heart once
destroyed,
As they are sent; I'll beam with joy.

Isn't this lovely?
To be happy.
Isn't this lovely?
To be me.

Every Story Needs a Villain

Thank you for showing me what I shouldn't
be,
Shrivelled skin and eyes so empty.
You were the worst role a model a boy
could ask for,
Always talking less but passively saying
more.
Do you know how many times I could see
through your mirror of manipulation?
You probably don't think I could; drowning
in self-absorption.
The day they told me you had gone,
I played my absolute favourite song.
Pop the champagne!
He's dead to me!

Every story needs a villain,
Here we fuckin' go again.
I thought your corpse was buried six feet
below;
So ignorant; little did I know;
That you were looming in wait to suck the

color from my life,
Holding a black and white Helvetica knife.
After all that you've done,
Do you really think you have someone, in
me?
I can't believe what I'm about to say is
true;
But I will never forgive you.

Resurrections brought on by my false sense
of security,
You can't just apologize to me; it's never
going to be that easy.
Funerals where the mourners do nothing
but smile,
Take the hint; hit the road; walk a mile.
Wake up at the wake;
Failed at your own game.
Coffins without corpses and men without
hearts,
Your blood makes wonderful paint for my
art.
Everybody grab a glass; I want to make a
toast;
That fucker is finally a ghost!

Every story needs a villain;
I was probably yours until the end.
Your kindness was a myth;
And your love; an urban legend.
Say goodbye to everything you once knew;
For I will never forgive you.
Whatever cosmic force writes my story
must have one heck of an imagination;
You have always been one vicious and
callous villain.
But my story is not one with a tragic end;
Sure, every story needs a villain;
But all I needed was a friend.
Right down to the wire; right at the end;
I hate to say I could never love you again.

Though we can never not be family,
You are now a stranger to me.
I'm leaving you in the dust and hoping
you'll rot,
It's time to focus on everything you are
not.
This story of mine has had a villain for far
too long;

I can save myself; a hero made to obliterate
what you've done wrong.

Into The Woods

Stories of love, damaged by disallowing
whispers,
"Are we enough?", we ask ourselves as we
disperse.
This city hustles like there's no time to rest,
Take my hand, replace manholes with
rabbit holes,
It's time we left.

Here I go into the woods,
I damn near didn't think I would.
Other people's opinions are nowhere to be
found,
I could scream and nobody would hear a
sound.
And you're here with me,
It's just us and a future history.
Now is our chance to dance a most
dangerous dance,
As we go into the woods,
We damn near didn't think we would.

Trees scrape the night sky like wire to a
palm,
I didn't realise chaos could be so calm.
The days are so peaceful, and the nights;
almost perfect,
Such a wonderful place to find myself, and
my love for you, it's worth it.
I'm no longer afraid of the dark,
In my change, you played a part.

Rainbows pierce my eyes through my
tears,
I haven't felt this confused in years.
It's like a sentence with no punctuation,
I don't know how I'm feeling.
Stuck in my ways,
Going insane.
Happy, sad and everything in between;
What the hell is happening inside of me?

Am I a psychopath?
Actually, no, don't answer that.
I can't see all the skeletons in my closet,
They're too real; if I confront them I'll lose
it.

Am I a perfect man?
Actually, no, don't answer that.
I can't see all the imperfections in me,
The comedown would be miraculously ugly.

Rainbows in June and flowers in bloom,
I've never felt this confused about you.
It's like a pen that doesn't write;
It makes no sense; it isn't right.
I don't know how I'm feeling,
A roll of film that just keeps reeling.
Stuck in my ways,
Going insane.
Happy, sad and everything in between,
What the hell is happening inside of me?

Before I met you my eyes withered with
self-oppression,
I couldn't answer life's most important
question.
Who are you?
I simply did not know.
Feeling blue but looking like gold.
You're the wind that made my wings fly,
I'm yours and you're my body type.

I'm so grateful for this enchanted forest,
It's serene, it's natural and it's perfect.

Here I go into the woods,
I damn near didn't think I would.
Other people's opinions are nowhere to be
found,
I could scream and nobody would hear a
sound.
And you're here with me,
It's just us and a future history.
Now is our chance to dance a most
dangerous dance,
As we go into the woods,
We damn near didn't think we would.

I'll race up my building's stairwell and
shout from the roof,
"I'M ABSOLUTELY, MADLY IN LOVE
WITH YOU!"
Stars in the night's sky will dim to focus on
me,
I am the embodiment of liberty.
I don't care who's listening; it's finally
time,

I can feel my heart beating; this love is
mine.
I'll kiss you on the streets with a smile on
my face,
These emotions were worth the wait.

I've found solace in open love,
And for that, I know I am enough.
I've found solace in open love,
And for that, I know I am enough.

We're Kids With Dreams Bigger Than This Town

My skin's been kissed by more than just the
sun,
Who's willing to be my next someone?
Everything's crumbling around me,
If I don't distract myself I know I'll end up
crying.
Delicate whispers of the day meeting the
ocean at dusk,
Rumors swirling around that something's
becoming of us.
Boomboxes blasting Rock N' Roll music
until all hours,
We're kids at the height of our powers.
Petals making homes in our palms,
The trees are way past bloom.
We're kids with dreams bigger than this
town,
Drowning, dying, decaying in this shrinking
room.
We need to have the summer of our lives,
So when winter comes and everything dies,

We can say we did this right.
Take my hand and follow me into the sun,
Make room for love, let's have some fun.

I haven't worn a shirt in six days,
Thanks to this almighty heatwave.
This house never did have an A/C machine,
Who knows what that means for me.
Maybe my secrets will melt into promises,
Turning perilous into positive.
Maybe I'll get struck down with
heatstroke,
And I'll regret what I stupidly spoke.
San Francisco's at the ready for when I
come crashing down,
I fear I'll never escape the talons of this
town.
I shake my head; this isn't the time to
think;
All I ever wanted was to be me.

I come home after a long day of doing
nothing;
Funny that; I also feel nothing.
I sit on the edge of my bed; I'm too afraid

to rest.
Will I ever be able to say I'm proud of myself?
Sure, I'm proud of the fact that I overcame
writer's block more times than I can count;
That I ate food even when my disorder
started to scream and shout;
That I avoided the brink of death twice;
That I have this ponderous ability to write.
But, is that enough?
What else is out there for me?
I know this is some deep, philosophical
stuff;
But, I'm just asking.
I might be a kid who's dreams are bigger
than this town;
But before I can leave I need to get to know
me for now.
One day you'll see my name lit up in lights;
And I hope you'll say;
Damn, he sure did everything right.

Roots Before Branches

Violets grow in the worst kind of violence,
There's something so sinister in this silence.
The rose garden dedicated to this city's
skyline;
It's slowly withering away; it's dying.
I can feel the heartbeat of this city below
my feet;
But I can't understand how I feel such
defeat.
Walls are closing in, palms are growing
sweaty;
Seduced into sin; I need to get away from
me.

Architecture is the bones of this city;
Every time I look at it; I feel a renewed
energy.
You can find me in New York City;
Where the boys are rebels and the girls are
pretty.
But I can't promise I'll be there for you;
It's a nice thought but I can't lie; I wouldn't

know what to do.
In a city full of billions of thoughts;
In mine; I've never been so lost.

There's always a seed before there's a rose.
The more that it rains, the more I will
grow.
I know today is the prologue to a whole
new world,
But I can't help but I feel like I'm lost for
words.
I feel like a version of myself is about to
die,
Struck down my something so different,
Something so vicious.
Change isn't something I ever thought
would scare me,
But, here we are, and this life of mine has
become incredibly overwhelming.

Waves of nostalgia pass over me as I
shiver;
I'm drowning in the Hudson River.
I can see Jersey City from here;
I hope everyone is happy over there.

I'll take a photo of this moment; only for
my eyes to see;
A kid so alone, here, in New York City.
I fought with someone I love so dearly;
What the *fuck* was I thinking?
I gaze at the photo I just took;
In the corner; he catches my eye; I take a
look.
A man sitting on a bench by the water;
His hat's covering his face but I know he's a
father.
I look closer at the shot;
I can see a faint tear; he too is lost.
I'm not the only one in New York City;
Everyone else's life is shitty!

Somehow that makes me feel less alone;
These roots before branches can only help
me to grow;
To grow into a man I can be proud of;
A man who can look in the mirror and
say; *You are enough.*
So meet me at dusk on 7th & 35th;
I'll take a Polaroid picture of you;
And you'll know that this is it.

Forest of Dreams

I have thorns in my side;
I bleed every night.
I feel two halves of a heart in my chest;
One beats; the other dies; it's relentless.
I wished upon stars for love my whole life;
I just didn't know it would let me know
how it feels to die.
I'm regretful for allowing myself to love;
I know how sad that sounds but I've had
enough.
I tried to say "I love you";
And I did say "goodbye",
Now, I don't know what to do;
Is there truth in this lie?

I've been sitting at my piano since dawn
broke,
I'm trying to find the words that should've
went unsaid.
Damn my naive tongue and all the words I
spoke,
It's about time I put my ego to rest.

I saw red last night and I'm sorry about
that;
The world is on my shoulders; it's breaking
my back.
I know I set your world alight;
Please, help me make this right.
Allow me to plant, in the ground, our
memories;
And, one day, we can get lost in our forest
of dreams.

I have roots growing out from the soles of
my feet;
Locking me in place; I can't make a move; I
can't breath.
It's true what they say; *You are your own
worst enemy*;
I'm sick and tired of my own villainy.
I want to love and I want to feel loved;
But maybe happiness is just down to luck.
If that's the case; then I'll forever be cold;
In this age; it's just me and the world.
God, I wish I was stronger to defy myself;
Maybe I need some kind of help.
I love myself, don't get me wrong,

But, I don't know who I've been loving all
along.

I've been sitting at my piano since dawn
broke,
I'm trying to find the words that should've
went unsaid.
Damn my naive tongue and all the words I
spoke,
It's about time I put my ego to rest.
I saw red last night and I'm sorry about
that;
The world is on my shoulders; it's breaking
my back.
I know I set your world alight;
Please, help me make this right.
Allow me to plant, in the ground, our
memories;
And, one day, we can get lost in our forest
of dreams.

I believe in magic;
A story written; tragic.
And I'll find myself in this forest of dreams;
It's the only way I'll ever truly know me.

Tangerine

I see orange in the most romantic of
sunsets,
The past twelve months have put me
through one hell of a test.
Beautiful scars could very well disappear by
your elegance,
An energy so pure, so heaven-sent.

I can take you to an island, tropi-ca,
I can feel you falling, exoti-ca.
Taste the bitterness of the tangerine,
Lead the way, make the hidden seen.
Taste the tangerine,
Taste the tangerine.

I see magenta when I hear the hollow
crackles of your voice,
Everyone tells me to forget about you, but
I don't have a choice.
We've been into the woods together,
And we can only keep those secrets between
us forever.

You know the darkest sides of me,
Sides of me I know aren't pretty.
I've said this once to you and I'll say it
again,
I'm slowly thinking you're becoming my
love and my best friend.

I can take you to an island, tropi-ca,
I can feel you falling, exoti-ca.
Taste the bitterness of the tangerine,
Lead the way, make the hidden seen.
Taste the tangerine,
Taste the tangerine.

You're lyrical,
You're mystical,
A godless fortuned fool,
But I'm so in love with you.

I can take you to an island, tropi-ca,
I can feel you falling, exoti-ca.
Taste the bitterness of the tangerine,
Lead the way, make the hidden seen.
Taste the tangerine,
Taste the tangerine.

American Dream

I'm angry, I can't lie;
I've been witnessing history all damn day.
Another soul down; how many more will
die?
Before this social plague goes away.
I fear it never will;
They'll always love the kill.
Maps guiding me to something close to
hope,
X's in the sand, a guidance to love.
All I'm trying to do is survive;
Survive this never-ending night.

Notes in lockers written with malicious
intent,
"I don't care about any of my friends".
Scars all over my body from attacks that
haven't happened yet,
Pain I know I'll pray to forget.
Reverbs of lies of what I could be,
I'm broken in this agony.

I am American made and royally fucked
up,
Always put my misfortune down to bad
luck.
I don't think I could ever fall in love,
Not when I'm too preoccupied with US.
I'm sorry;
Sorry that I don't believe in the American
dream,
I can feel it tearing at the seams.
Every river is flowing with the stars &
stripes of tears,
Red and blue in the streams.
Human pyramids at the border,
Cheerleaders in high school taking orders.
I don't believe in the American dream,
I can feel it tearing at the seams.

Watching TV all day in the hopes of
escaping,
I'll even watch *Riverdale* if it means not
thinking.
Listening to music and connecting with a
lyric so painfully,

It's like she wrote that song for me; so
eerily.

I'm sorry.
Sorry that I don't believe in the American
dream,
I can feel it tearing at the seams.
Every river is flowing with the stars &
stripes of tears,
Red and blue in the streams.
Human pyramids at the border,
Cheerleaders in high school taking orders.
I don't believe in the American dream,
I can feel it tearing at the seams.

Coast to coast all I see are ghosts,
Coast to coast I wish I could I see hope.
'Land of the free',
Oh, the irony.

I can hear *The Star Spangled Banner* play
briefly in the distance,
Drowned out by speeding, urgent sirens.
I think they paint the red in the American
flag with blood,

Wounded heartstrings, severely lacking in
love.
Some days I think that I've had enough,
A divisible nation, with no concept of trust.

I don't believe in the American dream.
I don't believe in the American dream.

Ghostwriter

Electric devotion and rays of light.
I can see clearly in the darkest of nights.
There's an eerie aura emitting from your
glow;
It's like your spirited kindness has nowhere
to go.
And I'm sad that we didn't get as far as
we'd like,
But shit like this happens all the time.
I can't sit around waiting for you to act,
This friendship isn't in tact.
I'm not saying I hate you or that I ever
will,
But I'm also not saying I love you; I'm far
too gone for him.

And he's writing emotional poems through
the coveted night;
I read them; I know it's not healthy, I often
ask myself why.
But I love reading poetry about me,
I adore words born out of agony.

I love reading poetry in my honor.
It makes me see that you still think I have
power.
I know, you know, you'd never admit it,
But you'd do anything to get back all up in
my business.
So carry on writing your poetry about me,
I'm the ghostwriter of every last word; I am
your artistry.

Paintings in my mind are the most
impressionistic of sorts,
Do you ignore me just for sport?
Rhythms in your poems are the most
romantic of types,
Would you say yes if I asked to speak with
you tonight?
Verses in my mind are the most classical of
such,
Is love a weapon or a drug?
Stories in your poems are the most abstract
of their kind;
Are these your words, or, are they mine?

Let me know when you have the answers to
those questions,
I'll be ready in waiting; flipping through the
pages.
There must be a word for the obsession we
share;
Was this born in lust, love, compassion or
care?
I'll haunt your pages until I know the
truth;
I am your ghostwriter, hiding between your
words; I am you.

Forever Again Pt. I

August 24, 2018:
So, this is it,
Wish I had known that was our last kiss.
I don't know when I'll see you next,
Just know you've been the best.
Summer's coming hot and fast,
How long does separation anxiety last?
You were the life of my party;
You had such a victorious energy.
I heard you dyed your hair blond recently;
I wonder how often you think of me.

There will come a time when you will see,
That you and I were always meant to be.
We will have our forever again,
I just don't know exactly when.
I know we haven't talked in what feels like
a year;
But your love will always have a home
here;
On the pages covered in my ink;
In the thoughts I love to think.

Stuck in a tailspin, a wild dance.
I can feel your presence on my skin, your
lingering lasts.
I hope to see you someday soon,
Your sun will caress my moon.
Until then, I'll wait forevermore,
Just for you to walk through my front
door.
I heard that you shaved your head
yesterday;
I wonder how often you remember me.

There will come a time when you will see,
That you and I were always meant to be.
We will have our forever again,
I just don't know exactly when.
I miss your neck;
I miss your arms.
I miss our texts;
I miss what was ours.

Forever Again Pt. II

June 6, 2020:

I wrote the verses above almost two years
ago;
And you're still very much on my mind.
Borderline stalker-ish;
Borderline obnoxious,
I'm writing this poem to let you know;
That you, well, you are one of a kind.
You're a talented musician;
I always wonder if I've ever been your
muse;
A musical addiction;
In your songs, have I ever been the 'you'?

I've seen you around on campus over the
last twenty-four months,
We've talked in passing a couple of times
and that just makes things worse.
You're about to start your career in the
spotlight;
I must confess; I listen to your songs every

night.
First loves leave a lasting impression;
You definitely did, my musician.
I wonder if we'll have our forever again;
Can former lovers graduate from being
friends?
The stars always seem to throw us together;
So, are you ready to try this again, forever?

Summer Stars

This town's lakes seem that much deeper,
Bargains in the corner shop seem that much
cheaper.
Colors are that much brighter when I'm
with you.
Senses are heightened; I don't know what to
do.
It's like you have a cause-and-effect on me,
I know that for a thousand percent
certainty.
This world is a better place with you in it,
please promise me you'll never leave it.

We can be summer stars just until the
autumn starts;
We can burn so bright that the whole world
sees our light.
Secrets are meant to be kept, keep me close
to your delicate chest.
We can be summer stars just until the
autumn starts;

Together for three months, forever and
never apart.

Auras are so much more fragrant, like
saturated lilies;
Tastes are incredibly different; like a
newfound beauty.
The world is a happier place when I'm with
you;
You make me see the world for it's truth; a
place of love, hope and eventual happiness;
A land on the path to a form of kindness.

Can we extend this summer fling?
I want to make this a concrete, real thing.
Shake my hand and lock in this deal;
I honestly can't believe love is real.
I see you in my dreams;
And I wake up with you next to me.
How the fuck did I get so lucky?
When did I get so happy?
I can see stardust and rainbows in your
eyes;
I'm enamoured by my illustrious type.

We can be summer stars just until infinity starts.
We can burn so bright that the whole world sees our light.
Secrets are meant to be kept, but ignore all that expose this.
We can be summer stars just until infinity starts;
Together for as long as we want, never, no, never apart.

Once in a Blue Moon

I can't make eye contact with strangers on
the street some days,
I hate that I always get stuck in my ways.
I stare at the ground until all of my sanity
is found,
And for that, I am not proud.
I wish I didn't find such respite in silence,
But I do, I adore the quiet.
That, I've known, could one day prove
problematic for me,
I could, simply, forget how to be.

I fall in love with you once in a blue moon,
I open up to you once in a blue moon.
Sixty years would be too soon,
I like drowning in my deepest solitude.
I let you in once in a blue moon,
I allow myself to be vulnerable once in a
blue moon,
It's always my sole voice in the room,
Loneliness finds the lonely in such gloom.

I'm not saying I'm down on my luck,
And I'm not telling you I'm stuck in a rut.
I'm just letting you know that vulnerability
is one of life's most complex entities.
In order to be vulnerable, you must be
completely honest with yourself,
And, to be honest, I don't think I'm there
yet.
I can tell everyone that I write what I feel,
But, deep down, I know this shit isn't real.
I know that I have problems that have
been swept under the rug,
I know that I can't always be so madly in
love.
What I'm trying to say is, I think, that self-
confidence and self-acceptance only come
once in a blue moon,
And, when it does, I promise I'll put them
to good use.

Okay

Agonising dreams of summer days that
always seemed to end,
The blood in my veins winces at things I
wish I said.
I hope you know all the memories are true,
I could never, ever forget about you.
What we had didn't just die,
Remember, there was no funeral.
It didn't just up and leave.
We both tried to be reasonable.
This love flew; it was free;
It's how it's meant to be.

And after all that we've been through,
You just say,
"Okay".
And you have no idea how perfect that was
to hear,
Hurting you fed my fear.
I didn't expect a smile so strong after all I
said was so wrong,
I've been feeling this way for so fucking

long.
To hear you say "*okay*" made me feel okay.

I painted some awful pictures in my mind
before that moment,
You stood above a dying version of me, my
chest was opened.
Your smile was tainted by my heart's
residue in your mouth,
I'd wake myself up to a deafening shout.
And I know none of that will ever or could
ever come true,
It's just nice to have that reassurance from
you.

And after all that we've been through,
You just say,
"*Okay*".
And you have no idea how perfect that was
to hear,
Hurting you fed my fear.
I didn't expect a smile so strong after all I
said was so wrong,
I've been feeling this way for so fucking

long.
To hear you say *"okay"* made feel okay.

Boy, do I have a story to tell.
I glanced down one rabbit-hole and I fell;
I fell harder than I ever have,
I fell further than I ever have.
Am amorcito under the summer skies,
I never knew love could be lacking in lies.
Boy, do you get me.
Boy, is this scary.
I think I'm ready.
Tell me you love me.

"Okay".

How Slowly They Wither

Fear is dead but nobody knows this yet.

An empty guitar case full of cash;
Hopes brutally, wistfully dashed.
I've been on the run like a convict for far
too long;
Every ounce of my humanity is absent; it's
gone.
I find myself in the middle of an
omnipresent desert;
An oasis of love; of all those feelings I've
remembered.
And in that mirage I can see a host of never
ending trees;
Like a continuous flow of what we know is
eternity.
I walk into nature with my heart on the
line;
Deceitfully telling myself that *everything's
fine.*

I feel minute in the middle of such glory;
A bohemian landslide; a fluorescent story.
It's the middle of July but each leaf has an
expiration date;
I can see browns, reds and yellows; for
some, it's already too late.
Oh, how slowly do the tides turn.
Oh, how slowly does the sun burn.
I'd do anything to feel free again;
I'd do anything to find a beginning in this
end.
Oh, how slowly does the cold shiver;
Would you look at how slowly they, and I,
wither.

Tell me you love me in such a natural
manner;
I'll be yours exclusively; yours forever.
I've peeled back layers upon layers of
myself in the last four months;
I've given myself one almighty chance at
growing up.
And that's all thanks to this world I've
created;
Where clouds float on waves and creativity

calms hatred.
To say goodbye is bittersweet;
Two worlds in one; embedded within me.
After all the time it took for these roots to
grow;
Finding solace in open love was the sign
only I could know.
I finally know who I am:
I know who I'm going to be.
A kid enamored totally and completely by
creativity.

In the storm I found the rainbow;
In the woods I found you.
In the pages I found the ability to let go;
In the branches I found what's true.

Thank you.